To Iris
our very best
and love from Angel
Derla + Mikey

Bill
Schaible

Darla, Mikey, and Their Angel

A True Story

Darla, Mikey, and Their Angel

A True Story

By William Schaible

The contents of this work including, but not limited to, the accuracy of events, people, and places depicted; opinions expressed; permission to use previously published materials included; and any advice given or actions advocated are solely the responsibility of the author, who assumes all liability for said work and indemnifies the publisher against any claims stemming from publication of the work.

All Rights Reserved
Copyright © 2023 by William Schaible

No part of this book may be reproduced or transmitted, downloaded, distributed, reverse engineered, or stored in or introduced into any information storage and retrieval system, in any form or by any means, including photocopying and recording, whether electronic or mechanical, now known or hereinafter invented without permission in writing from the publisher.

Dorrance Publishing Co
585 Alpha Drive
Suite 103
Pittsburgh, PA 15238
Visit our website at www.dorrancebookstore.com

ISBN: 979-8-88683-349-2
eISBN: 979-8-88683-327-0

Hello, my name is Angel and I'm a small, white Lhasa Apso dog. Even though I'm not a real angel, a couple of other small animals think I am.

My new mom and dad adopted me when I was only three years old. I belonged to another family after I was born, but I didn't get all the love and attention that a little dog should get. While home one night with my first family the front doorbell rang, so I couldn't wait to run and see who it was. It was a lady who I never met before, but she was friends with my first mom. This new lady said to me, "You are a very cute little dog." Then my first mom asked the new lady if she would like to adopt me because I wasn't very happy in my first home. The new lady said she would love to adopt me but had to ask her husband if it would be okay. Only one day later, the new lady and her husband decided they would love to have me as their pet, especially since this new mom and dad had no children or any other pets like me,

A couple of days later, my first mom took me for a ride and told me we were going to a new home, and I would have a new mom and dad to take care of me. My first mom carried me out of the car when we got to my new home, and we walked up the stairs to the front door of this new house. The doorbell was rang and I got to meet that new lady again, who was about to become my new mom. When I was put down on the floor of the new house, I could not wait to start looking around to see if I liked this new place. My new mom picked me up carefully and gave me a kiss on top of my head, and I thought, hold on a second, I'm not real sure I like you yet. My old mom and my new mom talked for a long time, and mostly it was about me. I heard them talk about how I was a nice, cute little dog, but I needed a new home because sometimes I made a mess on the floor because no one was home to take me outside to go potty. My old home sometimes had people visit, but these people were not nice to me and sometimes hit me when I did nothing wrong. I was still waiting to meet my new dad that night, but he was sick in bed, so when my old mom left, I finally

Angel in her new home with mom and dad.

got to see my new dad. My new mom was holding me kind of tight as we opened the bedroom door to see if my new dad was awake and if he wanted to see me. I was very nervous about my new dad and did not know if he would like me. He didn't feel well, but when he looked at me for the first time he became very happy and smiled.

My first full day in my new home was not scary at all because I liked all the room I had to run around and play. There was an upstairs and a downstairs, plus a backyard where I could lay down on the grass if I wanted. Also, my new mom and dad would let me sit or even sleep on the sofas; this was something I was not allowed to do at my old house. Mom and Dad didn't know that if I had to go to the bathroom that I would let them know. When we all went to bed that night, I was not allowed to go into the living room, dining room, the kitchen, or the hallway. I could only use the bedrooms and they all had towels on the floor. I guess this was in case I had to go to the bathroom, the towels were there for me to go on. After two weeks, Mom and Dad knew if I had to go to the bathroom, that I would scratch on the side of their bed and wake them up. I usually woke up my dad because I scratched on his side of the bed.

I heard my parents talking one day about getting a cam-corder so they could film me playing, walking in the park, or doing funny things. After just six months, they had more than 20 hours of movies for us to watch on T.V. Time went so fast and I was already in my new home a full year, and I was so happy here. Mom and Dad told me every day that they loved me. It seemed like every week I was going in the car for a ride to meet new people. All these people wanted to pet me and tell me how beautiful I was. I couldn't believe all the attention I was getting and how my life changed for the better.

Every day, I woke up in the morning, went to the bathroom, and then got to go on Mom and Dad's bed for two hours until Mom took me down. I had to come down because Dad went to work and Mom wanted to make the bed, which was so comfortable for me with two thick, soft blankets.

It was now time for me to visit the animal doctor for shots and a checkup. This was the only time I wasn't happy, and I would start shaking and get nervous. Mom or Dad were always with me when I had to see the doctor, and were close to me when the doctor had to look at my eyes, ears, and teeth. I also had to get shots that made me afraid, but they didn't hurt much at all. When the doctor handed me over to my dad, I knew we were going home, and I got so happy. Dad knew I was happy, and for being a good girl with the doctor, we went to get hamburgers on our way home.

After my dad knew that I loved to be around people, he began taking me to his office where he worked. The office had 36 people, and after two visits, I had met everyone. There were days when my dad was at work and my mom would take me to dad's office. I knew where I was just by remembering the parking lot, and then mom would let me run to the front door of the building.

Angel driving and in pool.

She let me in, and I knew exactly where to go to see Dad. While I was there, some other workers would come into my dad's office, and I got excited to see them again.

I always loved going for rides in the car but never knew where we were going. One day, Dad even let me try to drive by holding the steering wheel as I stood on his lap. Every day I got happier and happier with my new home and parents, but finally I had a sad day. I saw Dad go up into the attic and bring down suitcases. At first, I didn't think much of it, but the next day my parents told me they were going on vacation and would be back in six days. I got upset because I would be alone all that time, but just an hour later, a new man came to our house. He was my dad's father and I called him Grandpa. Grandpa was going to stay at our home and take care of me while Mom and Dad were on their vacation. I liked him right away, and he always let me sleep with him at night and watch T.V. with him on the sofa.

Angel's Halloween picture.

Before I knew it, my parents were back home, and they said thank you to Grandpa for taking good care of me. I love Grandpa, but I was so excited to see Mom and Dad again that I did a spinning dance on the floor that they called my happy dance! Only a week later, it was in the evening, I was lying on the sofa with Dad and our doorbell rang. Of course, I wanted to be the first one to the door, and when Mom opened it, there were four young kids on our porch. All night the doorbell rang again and again, and I was getting tired of running down the stairs to see who was there. I heard Mom and Dad say this night was Halloween. I did enjoy meeting all the new children, but the very young ones around four years old were afraid of me just because I wanted to sniff them.

   A few months later, my parents were spending a lot of time inside and outside the house putting up decorations. I had not seen this at my old house, so I didn't know what was going on.

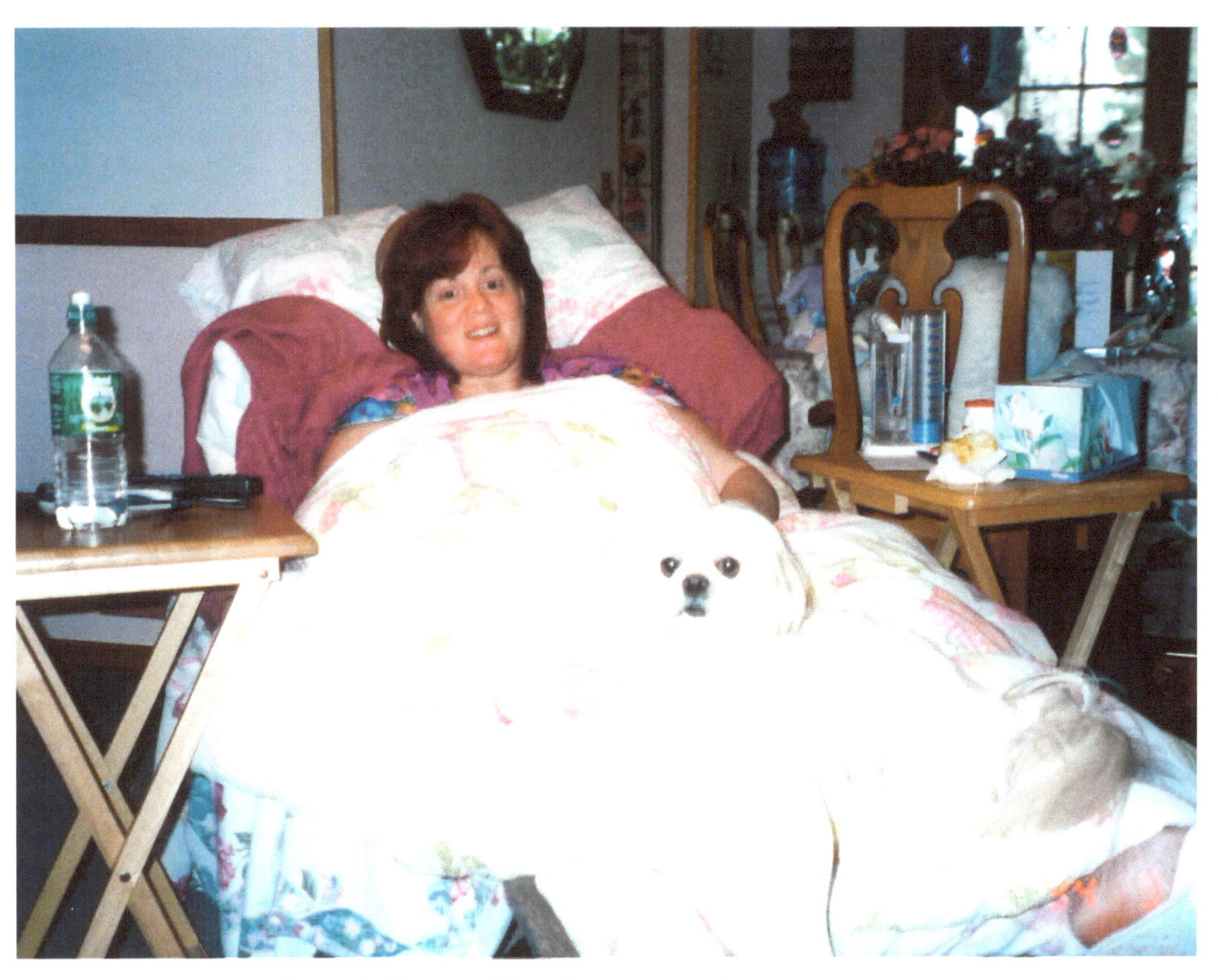

Angel "guarding" mom after surgery.

It turned out to be my favorite holiday, Christmas. There was a real nice green tree in our living room, big toys that moved and lit up, and also stockings hung near the T.V. with names on all of them, Mom, Dad, and Angel. My stocking was filled with my favorite treats like dog biscuits and Dingo bones. Only a month after Christmas my mom had to go to the hospital to have an operation. She was only gone one day but when she got home she was not able to move much and had to stay in a recliner chair most of the time. I didn't like the idea that mom was not feeling well so I stayed on the chair with mom almost all day to let her know I cared about her.

It was spring now and I always liked to sit in our living room bay window and look out at the whole street. One day I saw a cat outside in the street, and so I jumped all the way from the window to the floor and missed the sofa. When I landed, I hurt my left leg and sprained it. My parents had to take me to the doctor who gave me medicine to take for a whole month.

Baby cottontail - Little Guy
Dad feeding the baby bunny

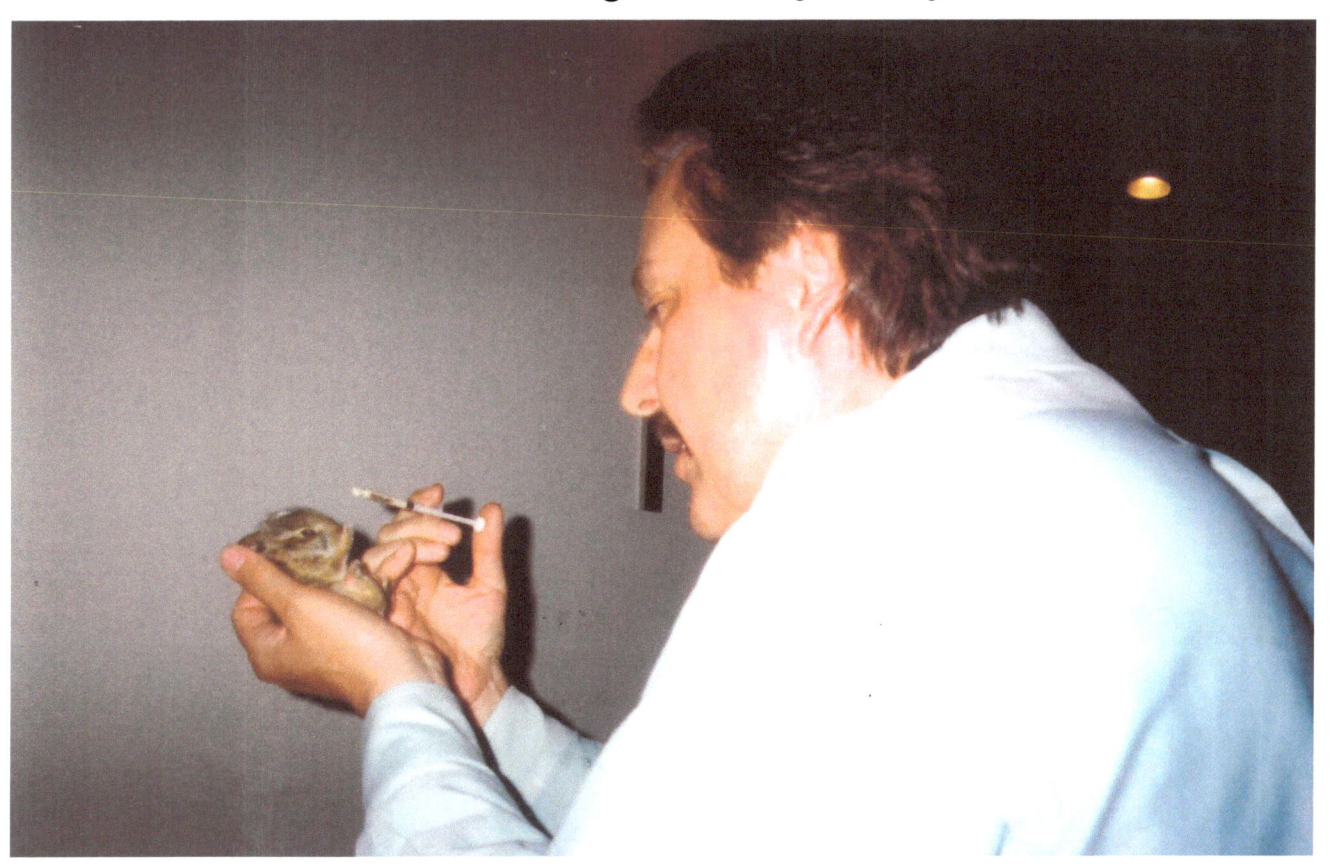

I couldn't do anything for many weeks because my leg hurt so much. I didn't go for a haircut either, and my fur was getting very long and sloppy.

Five weeks later I was finally feeling better, and I could walk down the stairs by myself with no help from Dad. That following Saturday, my dad had to work for two hours, so he took me with him to the office. After one hour I started getting bored and wanted to leave. Dad told me, "Just a few more minutes, Angel." We were leaving the front door of the building when I went over to a flower bed to go to the bathroom. My dad said, "No Angel, not there," so I walked around to the grass and near a small tree. My dad was wondering what was taking me so long because I saw something strange, and Dad came over to see too. I had just found a nest in the ground of baby cotton-tail rabbits! There were five of them and no sign of their mother. They were kind of afraid of me but too scared to run away. My dad went to work for an hour the next day too, and he said the baby rabbits were still in their nest.

That night there was a bad thunderstorm, and I was worried about the baby rabbits getting wet and not being able to hide. The next morning was Monday, and Dad went back to work, but the first thing he did was check on the babies. All the babies were gone except for one. Dad took that baby bunny inside and made sure he (we called him Little Guy) was safe and dry. Dad called a couple of animal doctors to see what was good to feed him. The little guy had to be fed kitten formula because he was too little for regular food. Mom was on vacation with her family in Italy, so she didn't get to meet the little rabbit until two months later. Dad wanted to keep him until he was old enough to live at a place where alot of other animals like racoons, squirrels, possums, and other rabbits live. He lived in a large box in the dining room and was fed the formula from an eye dropper that he seemed to really like. I wanted Dad to let me play with the bunny, but he said no because I might scare him too much.

Each week he grew more and more, and now he was eating lettuce and drinking water, so we had a good feeling he was going to be okay. Dad was wondering what happened to the rest of the baby bunnies and why our Little Guy was left behind. Mom was only a week away from coming home from Italy, and Dad decided to give Little Guy to the place that could take care of him better. We missed him very much, and Dad was thinking about getting a real house bunny, because we are not allowed to keep wild rabbits and that's what Little Guy was. Dad and I drove to a few pet shops looking to buy a new rabbit, but all the stores said they don't sell rabbits anymore and we had to try a rabbit shelter. A girl at one of the pet stores gave my dad a list of bunny shelters, and so he called the first number.

The shelter asked him what breed of rabbit he wanted and he wasn't sure, but told them a rabbit not too big and not too small. This shelter had seven rabbits, all three months old, and all were a breed called mini-rex, except for one which was an English Spot.

Darla and Mikey 1 year old.

Dad couldn't wait to drive down to the shelter and adopt one of these rabbits. I wanted to go for the ride but it was far, and Dad didn't think it would be a good idea. When Dad got to the shelter, a woman asked him if he wanted a girl or boy rabbit and he said a boy. There was a real big cage with all seven rabbits inside and the woman said that the boy rabbit he wanted was a black mini-rex that she pointed to. Five of the bunnies were all the way down at one end of the cage and the other two were at the other end. When the woman tried to pick up the bunny the white bunny came over and tried to stop her. That's when my dad said he will take both of them which turned out to be a very good thing. Dad got home about three hours later, just in time to take me outside to the bathroom and came home with two rabbits and not just the one that he wanted in the first place. I got to meet the two bunnies who were now going to share the house with me. I didn't like that at first but they were so cute and friendly that I didn't want to be selfish. Mom got back home from her vacation and got a big surprise, two beautiful little rabbits.

Darla and Mikey outside eating.

One was black and one was white with gray spots and this one was a girl, so they were brother and sister. The black one (Mikey) could not move two steps without Darla following right with him. They soon became very close friends with Mikey always trying to protect his sister, Darla. My dad wasn't sure how to take care of rabbits the right way because he never had bunnies before as pets, but he was always reading about rabbits on the computer and bought books too.

My mom and dad didn't think a cage was the right home for the two rabbits, and after one year, they had a new place to live in the house, their own big bedroom! While they were in their cage, Mikey didn't like anyone sticking their hands inside or he would bite. My dad was told that boy rabbits protect the home, and in this case, he was protecting his sister too. During their only winter in the cage, which was in the garage and not very warm, Mikey always put himself on top of Darla to keep her warm.

Now with their new, big warm room, Mikey didn't have to do that anymore. Every time Dad went downstairs to check on Mikey and Darla I followed

Angel in her new yard.

Angel first outside meeting with Darla.

him down so I could at least see them and sometimes even play with them. Mikey wasn't much for playing with me, and Darla usually pretended she didn't even see me and would eat her hay instead. The next year, Dad built an outside pen in the backyard for Mikey and Darla so now except for the winter had another big place to run, play, and relax. The outside pen was almost thirty feet long and Dad put a hutch inside the pen so they could hide or just get out of the sun. It was only a month later, and Darla escaped from the pen and left Mikey alone to wonder what happened to his sister and if she were alright.

Dad and a friend found Darla in a neighbor's yard under a porch where she looked scared, because it was a place she didn't know very well. We were all so happy to have Darla back, but probably not as happy as Mikey, her best friend. Every time Mom let me out in the backyard to go to the bathroom, I had to go over and try to play with Mikey and Darla, but could not get into their pen without someone lifting me and putting me in.

Dad and Mom were against the idea of me in the pen with the bunnies because they thought I might get too rough with them. A month later in September, Mom decided to put me in the pen with the rabbits to see what would happen. Only a few seconds after being put inside the pen, Mikey and Darla came running over to me and started sniffing and kissing me. I thought they might gang up on me and even bite me, but they were very friendly and didn't mind me being in their play area. Now winter was coming again, and the rabbits would no longer use their outside pen. It would be too cold for them because house rabbits don't like weather under 40 degrees, so now they would stay inside the house in their own room until the spring.

By now, I was getting to know Darla and Mikey very well, and I could tell that Mikey was shy but strong, not as smart as Darla, didn't mind sharing his treats with his sister, and wasn't much for adventure. Darla was not shy at all and liked to be the boss. She also would never sit still while outside in the pen, and was always looking for a way to escape the pen and explore the rest of the backyard. Darla would also take Mikey's treats away from him, and many times, take the treats right out of his mouth. He would never get mad at Darla for doing this and would just hop over to Dad and ask for another treat. Mom and Dad always gave me about ten minutes each day where I could play in the rabbit's room with them and watch them eat their green vegetables. The funniest was watching them eat parsley because they would suck it up like they were eating spaghetti. I didn't like the food they ate because rabbits don't like food such as chicken, hot dogs, hamburgers, and fish. They eat a lot of hay but also like lettuce, Brussel sprouts, kale, and spinach. Each of them had their own water bowl and their own litter box like the kind cats use. Just like me, Darla and Mikey would sometimes have to go see the doctor. Usually just a checkup, but once in a while one of them would get hurt while playing too hard and hurting a leg or something. Dad and I knew when one of them was not feeling well or was hurt, because they would sit in the same place for a whole day and not move at all. Dad would bring them to the doctor just in case to make sure it was nothing bad. One day, Dad went into their room to feed them and I went in too to see my best friends. Mikey was sitting right near the bedroom door, and he never does that. I went over to say hello to Darla, but she was in a corner of the room and would not move. That's when Dad and I knew something was bothering her. We think Mikey knew Darla was not well and was trying to leave the room and get help. Mom and Dad brought her to the doctor that afternoon. Mikey and I went along for the ride and also to show Darla that we cared for her and were worried. The doctor said she had an upset stomach, and with a little medicine, she was better the next morning.

Spring arrived again so it was time for me, Mikey, and Darla to spend a lot of time outside. One April morning, Dad brought the bunnies outside to their pen then he and I went back in the house. About two hours later, we went out to give them a few treats, and again Darla was not in the pen and escaped again! She dug a hole under the fence of the pen, and we could not find her anywhere. We looked for over an hour but there was no sign of Darla. Then I heard my dad say to Mikey, "I think you're all alone now, big guy." Many hours went by and still no Darla, and I was getting very sad that I might never see my friend again. It was now past dinner time, and we still could not find Darla. Mom and Dad had very sad looks on their faces and things looked bad. Before it got dark, Dad took me out in the backyard to go to the bathroom when I thought I heard a soft noise coming from the back corner of the yard. I started to head that way when Dad said, "No, Angel, you have to come inside." I didn't want to disobey Dad, but I ran off to the where I heard the noise. Would you believe it? I found Darla digging a hole in a mound of dirt behind our shed. I barked and Dad came running over to find Darla head-first inside the hole. He quickly pulled Darla out and hugged her as I saw tears running down my dad's cheeks.

Mikey was back inside the house the whole day because Dad didn't want him to escape too, and when he saw Darla, he hopped over very fast to her and kissed her nose. He might have thought that he may never see his sister again since the two of them were never apart. My mom and dad were so proud of me for finding Darla, and wanted to thank me with a fresh piece of cooked salmon for dinner.

You see, Mikey and Darla always considered me their own "Angel from Heaven" because if I had never found that baby rabbit in the nest three years earlier, my dad would not have the idea of adopting another rabbit, or in our case, two rabbits. They may never have been adopted and had a nice home with caring parents who loved them a lot.

That next summer, it was very hot and Mikey, Darla, and I did not stay outside very long each day. One day that was not that hot, I saw Dad put the rabbits out in their pen around 9 o'clock in the morning. I would always follow Dad wherever he brought them to make sure everything went well. That night, it had just gotten dark, and that's when Dad always brough Mikey and Darla back in the house. Rabbits don't really like the dark and it makes them a little scared. Dad and I went out the backdoor, across the patio, and into the grass where the bunny pen was. Before Dad could step into the pen to get them, I counted three animals and not two. Who or what was this extra animal? Dad got very nervous because he said to me the third animal was a skunk, and the rabbits could maybe get sprayed with stinky stuff. If they got sprayed with the skunk stuff, Darla and Mikey might have to go to the hospital that same night! Dad said the skunk was still a baby and that was a good thing. The rabbits usually didn't want Dad to bring them in until they are ready, but this time Dad hoped they would let him pick them up fast and get into house. The skunk went into the rabbits' hutch-type house and we thought this was the perfect time to get Darla and Mikey out before we saw the skunk again. Dad went to pickup Darla and she ran into the hutch, and the same with Mikey. "Oh no," said Dad, "not that!" He was sure the skunk would spray the bunnies, but he didn't.

Angel with dad on boat.

In just a few seconds, Mikey and Darla came running out and right to Dad. He picked up both of them, and all four of us ran back in the house. Dad went back outside and tried to get the skunk to leave by taking down some of the pen, and thankfully he did leave. Dad had also opened the door of the fence that surrounded the whole backyard, and the skunk was completely gone now and ran down the street. That was a really close call because all of us could have gotten pretty smelly.

A couple of weeks later in late July, Mom and Dad said we were going to see friends who had a house at the shore and a boat. I got really excited because I had never been on a boat before or anywhere near the ocean. It was a hot day, so Mom brought plenty of water for me and a bowl. The boat actually had a downstairs area and I stayed there most of the time to get out of the hot sun. We were on the boat for about two hours and stopped once so the adults could swim in the water. The water scared me a little, so the daughter of the friends stayed with me and kept me company. That was a fun day for me, but I was a little unhappy that Mikey and Darla could not come.

Darla with some of her 1st place prizes..
Darla and Mikey winning photo - cutest eating.

By late summer, I would stay outside in the backyard and keep my eye on the rabbits while they played in their pen. I stopped to get a drink of water, and when I went back, Darla was very scared and not moving at all. She was also pounding her back legs into the ground, and it made a funny sound. Just then, I knew why she was scared, a cat was in our yard and only ten feet away from Darla outside the pen. I didn't think the cat would hurt the rabbits, but Darla was afraid, so I chased the cat out of the yard. Dad heard me barking and ran outside to see the cat running away and now Darla was okay again.

One Saturday in October, Dad and Mom were bringing Mikey and Darla to something called a rabbit show an hour drive away. The show had some people bring their rabbits for others to see and many other people were there to sell rabbit stuff. Most of the bunny owners entered a photo contest the week before, and this was the day the winners were announced.

35

Another bunny won third prize and then another pretty bunny won second prize. When they said Mikey won first prize, Mom and Dad were very happy and surprised, but even more when Darla was declared grand prize winner! I wish I was there to see this, but I did see all the gifts that they came home with. What a great day that was and we were all very proud of Mikey and Darla.

I was spending so much time with Mikey and Darla that Mom and Dad would leave the door open in the rabbits' bedroom so I could go in and see them any time I wanted. One afternoon, I was just relaxing in the bunny room and saw Mikey go over and try to rub noses with Darla. She would always kiss him back or hop away, but this time she did not move. Since I'm an animal too, I got a bad feeling something was wrong with Darla. I went upstairs and scratched Dad on the ankle to get his attention. I usually do this when I have to go to the bathroom, but this time I ran into the rabbits' room and walked up to Darla. My dad also thought something was wrong and we all went into the car for a ride to the doctor.

Enjoy the Holiday Season

Mikey & Darla

Christmas card photos

37

The nice doctor spent over fifteen minutes with Darla while the rest of us waited. Then the doctor said that Darla had something wrong with her liver, but we found out in time to help Darla get better in four days.

Remember I said that Christmas was my favorite holiday? Well, Mom and Dad love it too and decided that Mikey, Darla, and I would have a photographer take our picture to use for a Christmas card. I love having my picture taken and now it was for a greeting card, so I was on my best behavior. We had Christmas card photos taken eight times, and once was at a pet store where people were bringing in their big dogs also for Christmas cards. Darla, Mikey, and I were on the floor in the store with Christmas stuff around us like presents and flowers. When I saw big dogs coming into the store, I became afraid for Mikey and Darla because these dogs were so much bigger than they were. I wasn't scared because I knew Dad would protect me, but if the bunnies were scared and tried to run away that the big dogs would chase after them.

Mikey and Darla at Childrens Hospital fundraiser.

Well, the four dogs did a lot of barking, but Mikey and Darla did not move an inch and actually stayed still until all the pictures were taken. When we got home later, Dad gave all of us our favorite treats for being such good sports.

The winter was over and it was a warm middle of March when my dad got a call at work from a woman named Nancy who my mom and dad met a year earlier. She wrote a nice book about her family and their rabbit, "Bunny Boy." This woman helped out a lot with a children's hospital, and three years in a row brought her rabbit to a hospital fundraiser and concert to help kids. All the kids were able to see, hold, and pet her girl bunny named Muffin. Nancy was planning on bringing Muffin to the concert again, but she became ill and could not go. When Nancy called my dad, she asked him if Mikey and Darla could go to the children's hospital instead of Muffin to make the kids happy. Dad said yes, and the next week, Mom, Dad, a friend Edy, Mikey, Darla, and Nancy went to the concert. Dad said it would be better if I did not go because it would be a long night for me.

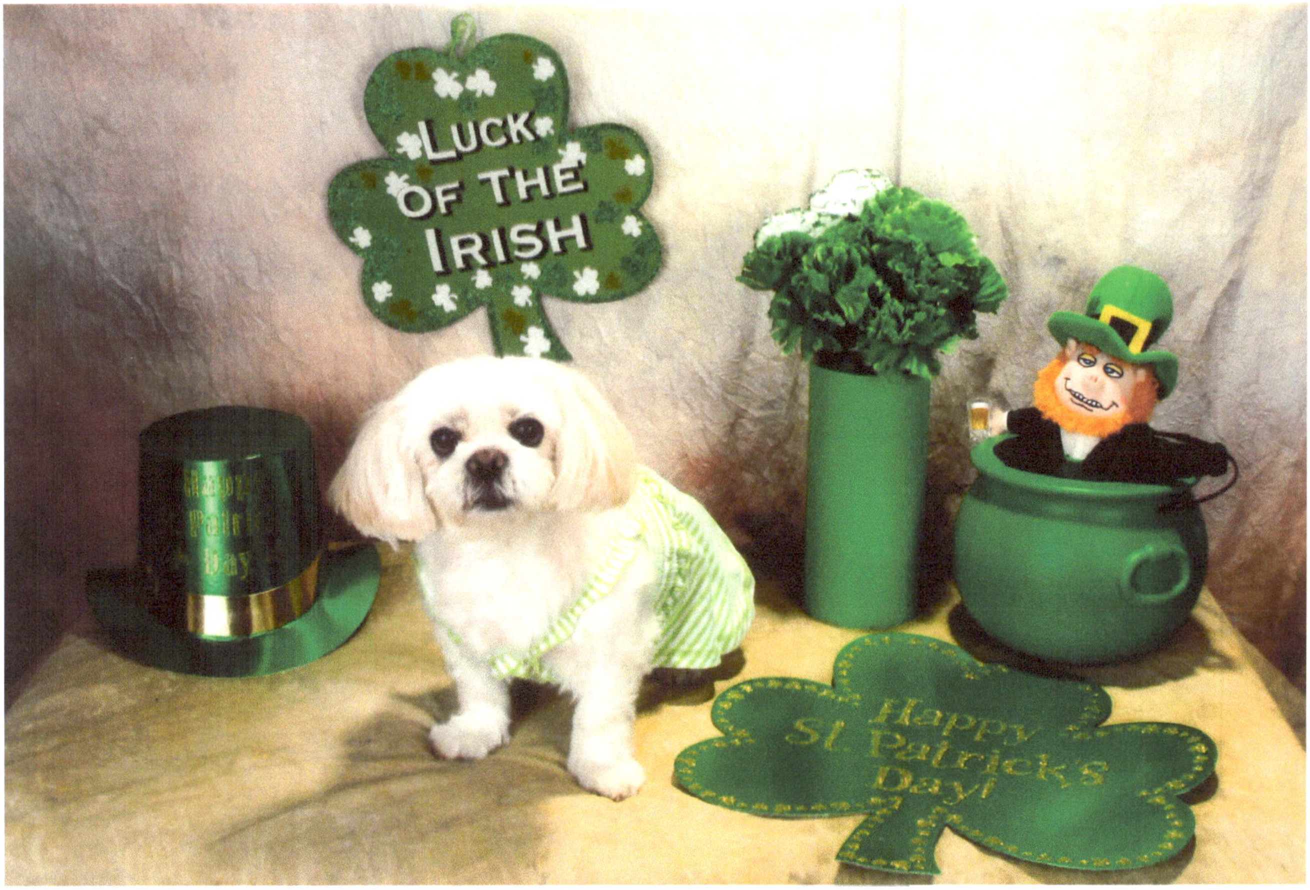
LUCK OF THE IRISH
Happy St. Patrick's Day!

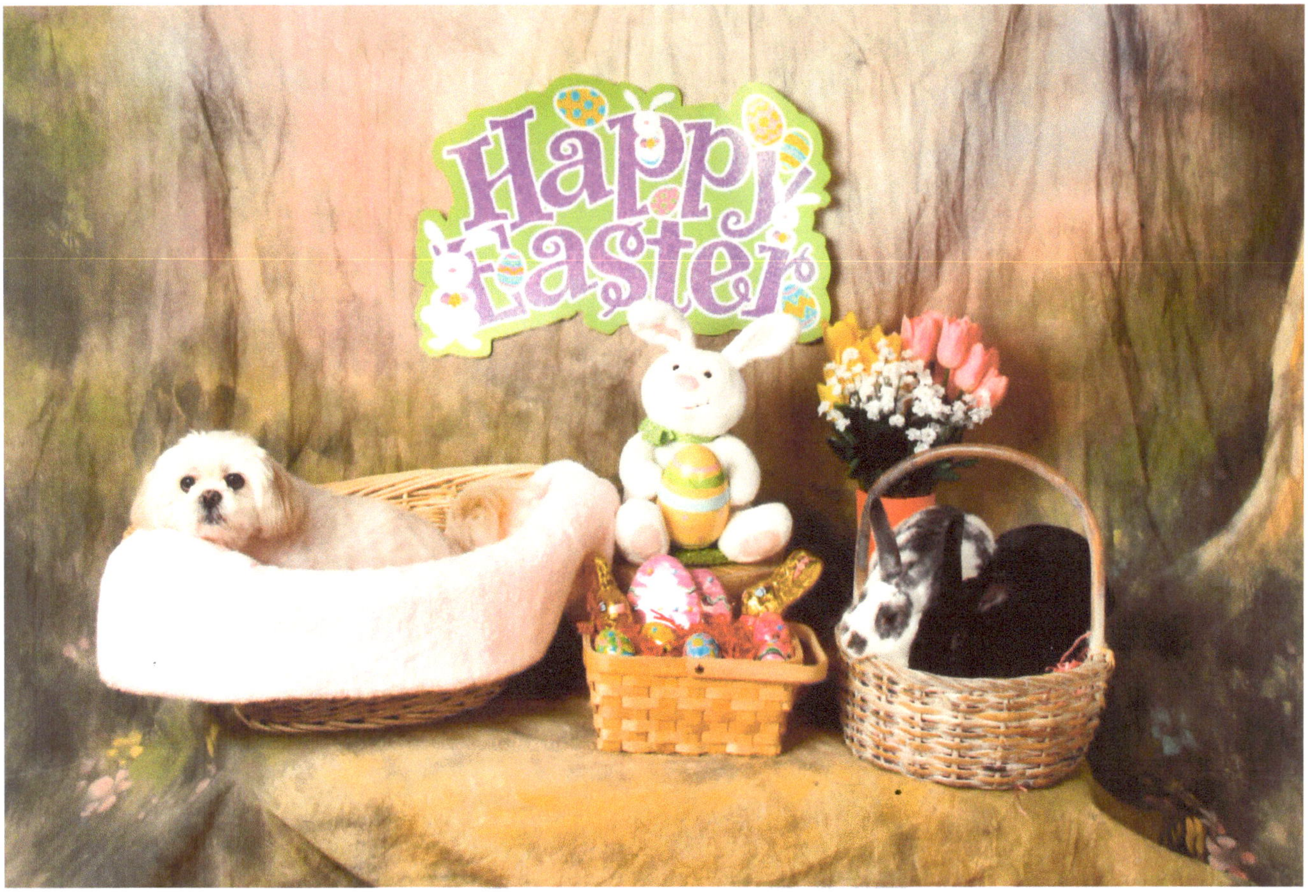
Happy Easter

Inside the hospital, there was a big hallway outside the concert room where they waited at two tables before the children started to arrive. Darla and Mikey were in their carrier with the top off on one of the tables. There must have been more than 100 kids that came that night all between ages five and twelve, and many of them got to hold Mikey and Darla, and even had pictures taken with them. There was even a photographer there from the town newspaper. It was a long, noisy night for the bunnies, but they were not afraid at all and loved being held by all the kids. They finally started home after the concert ended around 9:30 at night, and when Mikey and Darla got inside the house, they each ran fast to the two litter boxes to go potty. Then a long drink from the water bowl, a goodnight kiss from Mom and Dad, plus a lick on the back from me.

The next year, Dad made a video of the rabbits and me that you can watch on YouTube. All I can say is I wasn't a real good girl that day, but you can watch for yourself. (Rabbit vs. Lhasa)

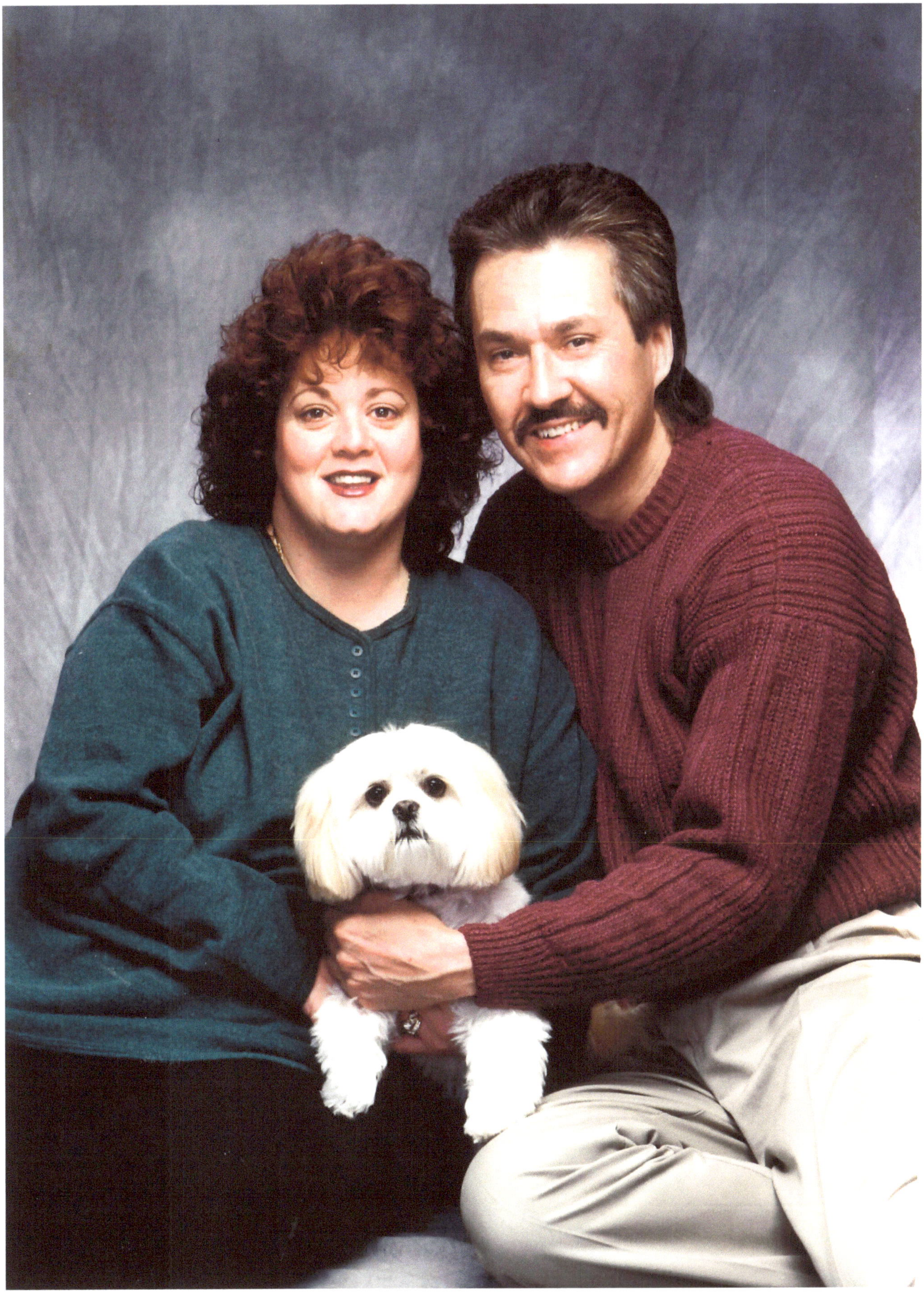

Thank you for reading my book. Your friend, Angel

I can't believe I've been a big sister to Mikey and Darla for 11 years. We've had so much fun together and a lot of happy times, but a few sad times too like when we didn't feel well and Darla kept escaping from the pen. But we are always there for each other and hope that never ends. I'm older now and my legs hurt sometimes, so Mom and Dad have to help me up and down the stairs to go outside. They don't mind at all because they love me, and I love them for giving Mikey, Darla, and me such a wonderful home. A home I wish every pet could have! I won't ever forget my two wonderful friends and they will always remember me as "their Angel."

Dedicated to:
William C. Schaible, Phyllis R. Schaible, and Karen Ostrander Schaible.

Special thanks to:
Connie Schaible (Mom)
Best Friends Animal Society, Kanab Utah
Safe Haven Rabbit Rescue, Clinton, NJ
Luv-N-Buns Rabbit Shelter, Philadelphia, PA
Brambley Hedge Rabbit Rescue, Phoenix, AZ
Tribbles Corp.
ASPCA
Community Animal Hospital, Morris Plains, NJ
Denville Animal Hospital, Denville, NJ
All Creatures Great and Small, Fairfield, NJ
Nancy Laracy
Edy Toussaint
NJSCPA, Roseland, NJ
Parsippany, NJ
OEM